Higher Consciousness

Finding Peace and Joy
Above the Noise

Owen Waters

Copyright ©2020
Infinite Being LLC, USA
ISBN 978-1-932336-41-2

Published by Spiritual Dynamics Academy LLC
www.SpiritualDynamics.net

First published: November 2, 2020
All rights reserved.

Table of Contents

Introduction

In a world filled with intense conflict, can you really rise above it all? Can you really find peace and joy above the noise and clatter of politics, steaming resentment and even hatred that circulates today?

The answer is yes, definitely... *if* you know how. This book will provide you with that exact information. You also need to be prepared to remind yourself each day of your true spiritual nature in order to insulate yourself from the constant daily supply of negative conditioning that typically comes with life on earth today.

The good news is that all things come to pass and today's atmosphere of negativity is especially fated to pass away. As I will explain later in this book, a new dawn is coming to Planet Earth. The ground beneath your feet, your entire body, and everything in this physical world is about to rise in frequency. After this event, which future generations will simply refer to as the culminating event of *The Shift*, conflicts will be resolved with ease instead of anger. A load will be lifted from the minds of everyone on the planet. No one will be left behind in The Shift. The planet will vibrationally ascend, taking us along for the ride into a wonderful New World of higher existence.

The more you focus upon higher consciousness today, the sooner the world will be ready to "rise in the heavens." You may feel that you are just one person among billions of people but, as you will learn later in this book, your efforts at moving into higher consciousness can affect *thousands*, and even *hundreds of thousands*, of other people, making the way forward for them easier because you helped prepare the way.

While higher consciousness is primarily accessed through the feelings of the heart, there is also a science which supports your curiosity as to how you can achieve a life of joyful existence.

Think of human consciousness as existing upon a vibrational scale, rather like a musical scale. Each note or level has its own unique sound frequency. The most familiar *scale of consciousness* to people today is called Maslow's Hierarchy of Needs in Human Motivation.

Maslow listed the basic stages of the journey of human progress starting with basic and psychological needs, then progressing through self-fulfillment and on to the ultimate human reward of transcendence.

Maslow's Hierarchy

There are five stages of Maslow's Hierarchy of Needs commonly taught in college classes. Maslow included an additional sixth stage of Transcendence but most professors haven't yet caught up with such inspired insights. Here are the full six stages.

1. Physiological needs - food and shelter
2. Safety needs
3. Social belonging
4. Self-esteem
5. Self-actualization - achieving one's potential
6. Transcendence - an inner, spiritual awakening

With its six stages of consciousness, we can refer to this original list as "Maslow-6."

Maslow Predicted A Major Shift

Abraham Maslow (1908-70) was a psychologist who became well known for this hierarchy of human needs. When he developed his theory in the 1940s, he predicted the transformation of humanity into a realm of spiritual transcendence, but he had no idea just how soon this would develop into a major movement.

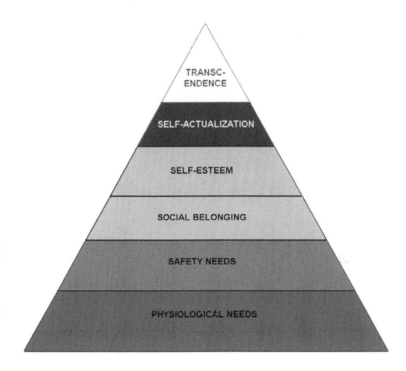

Maslow's Hierarchy of Human Needs shows that basic human needs have to be fulfilled before people can attend to higher needs and values.

First, the basic physiological needs of food and shelter must be catered for in order to ensure survival.

Second, once food and shelter are obtained, safety and security must be achieved.

Third, acceptance by others is sought, in both the societal and personal senses. To fulfill this 'belonging' need, people become part of a group, a tribe, an extended family or a community.

When these deficiency, or outer-directed, needs are satisfied, then the individual works to acquire self-respect. Recognition by others produces self-esteem.

Once the outer needs are fulfilled, the inner-directed need for self-actualization comes into play. To self-actualize means to become the best you personally can be. Self-actualized people include those who have achieved material abundance, and also those who, as a decision of personal power, have chosen simplicity over the pursuit of further abundance. At some point, when a person says "That's enough" to the endless pursuit of additional financial security, then they become free to accomplish anything that inspires their inner joy the most.

Self-actualization is achieved after the individual ceases to have deference to hierarchical authority, and instead matures into the ability to make their own rules of personal responsibility. Personal responsibility is always more powerful and effective than any system of imposed rules. For example, you can threaten to punish someone if they steal and hope that the threat works. But, a self-responsible person simply wouldn't steal because they would feel empathy for the loss that a would-be victim would feel.

Self-actualized people no longer need external rules to mold their behavior because they simply don't have the heart to hurt other people.

It's a matter of increased maturity. When a person abandons the impositions of external authority and becomes their own, self-directed authority, then they become far more functional in the world. This is a higher state of consciousness - one which provides a higher vista of awareness. From this expanded vista, they see clearly how they as an individual can best serve humanity.

In this state of awareness, the person acquires the ability to think and analyze situations independently. As a result, new and creative solutions spring to mind. They have enough self-esteem to be able to clearly see their own needs, skills, strengths and weaknesses, and from that they see where they can best be of service to humanity.

Once basic needs are fulfilled, the next values to require attention relate to being. The first of these being-values is self-actualization, which is the instinctual need of a human to make the most of their unique abilities.

Above that, Maslow placed transcendence, which he considered a spiritual value. The being-values of self-actualization and transcendence are the higher, more beautiful aspects of human consciousness. They include unconditional love, altruism, inner joy, a love of nature, the development of intuition (in males as well as females), idealism, and a sense of wisdom which springs from within. These skills develop the right-brain functions of creativity and intuition.

In the 1950s, Maslow believed that only 2% of the population had achieved self-actualization. The mid-1960s changed all that when masses of people began the search for the higher values, such as unconditional love and spiritual wisdom. Today, that core group of progressive people has blossomed from 2% to well over 26% of the population, and it is climbing every year.

The Shift is not a temporary by-product of the baby boom generation, or any other generation of modern culture. It is not a passing fad. It is not going away. It is a cosmic pressure that is unfolding and relentlessly increasing the frequency of all consciousness upon the planet.

It is a part of the plan of the Creator that we progress to the next stage of conscious human achievement. The Shift is, to put it simply, the most wonderful transformation in recorded history. This is where humanity gets to build, literally, Heaven on Earth.

New Insights Since Maslow

Maslow's Hierarchy was published in 1943. Since then, other psychologists and social scientists have weighed in upon the subject, carrying out extensive surveys in order to clarify the stages and possibly fill in any gaps.

Clare W. Graves (1914-86), was a pioneering social scientist who independently identified the historical phases of civilization and social progress. To his surprise, he came to a realization that, today, mankind is preparing for a momentous leap. This leap, he said, would be a mega-change in society which would dwarf all previous changes.

Clare W. Graves was a professor of psychology at Union College, New York. In the chaotic years after World War II, he wanted to determine exactly what lies beneath human nature. Rather than comparing the conflicting theories of the day, he decided to dump them all, right in the trash can! Then he decided to figure out for himself what was happening. Graves, unfortunately, passed away in 1986, just before releasing the book which would have expanded greatly upon his life's work.

Two of his students, Don Beck and Christopher Cowan, stepped in to fill the void caused by his departure. They assembled and published the essence of his research in their 1996 book, Spiral Dynamics. In it, Beck and Cowan have taken Graves' theory even further, enhancing his findings by drawing from the science of Memetics, the study of memes.

Memes are the social equivalent of genes, cultural units of information which self-replicate from mind to mind on a vast scale, appearing within society as new trends of thought. So far, eight different memes have been identified and analyzed in the evolution of society throughout recorded history.

The different memes, which reflect the evolution of society from its primitive beginnings up to the present, are defined by the following keywords from the perspective of Spiral Dynamics.

1. Basic survival. The most primitive motivation of just staying alive.

2. Clans. Tribal and family bonding along with superstition-filled attempts to understand the powers of nature which threaten to overpower them.

3. Survival of the fittest. Mastering the environment, fighting to break constraints. Sensing many gods, all of which are models of power. After all, from their tribal point of view, a lightning storm would mean that something pretty big up there must be angry about something.

4. Finding purpose in life. Obeying authority and rules of morality, sacrificing the self to a greater cause for a deferred reward. Dedicating allegiance to one supreme God.

5. Striving to succeed. Fighting to win, beating the competition, pursuing intellectual development, achieving independence.

6. Community and caring. Unconditional love, accepting others as they are, seeing the value of service to others, caring for the environment, seeding the beginnings of spiritual understanding.

7. Flexible flow. Big-picture views, the discovery of self-accountable, personal freedom. This is the level of self-actualization where personal purpose comes into focus.

8. Global view. Spiritual awareness, learning through simply being as well as doing, becoming conscious of the superconscious, developing deeper intuition.

Clare Graves saw the first set of six memes as a first tier of human development. He called the transition of the human race to meme number seven a momentous leap, an entry into an entirely new set of memes, or tier of consciousness.

With this new tier comes freedom from all of the fears of the prior memes, and, finally, the freedom for human cognition to focus upon its possibilities in the world. In meme number seven, people act from an inner-directed core. Values come from fundamental, natural law, meaning that human rights are perceived as fundamental due to the fact that you exist.

By nature, seventh meme thinkers are self-accountable and independent within reason. They are honest in their communications and do not spend time on the rules of formality, unless they are important to those present. Seventh meme thinkers like technology for what it can do to improve life, and they value knowledge and competency above rank or status.

They enjoy the pleasures of life, without being bound by any of them, and pursue activities that express their inner joy. External fashions and trends have no bearing upon these choices. They have emotional control, meaning that they still express emotions, but these expressions are appropriate, and not uncontrolled outbursts.

Maslow Updated

Based upon the discoveries made in the Spiral Dynamics material, we are now able to add two new stages to the six stages of the original Maslow's Hierarchy, filling out the scale of human consciousness in a more complete manner. The terminology of the two systems may differ, but the fundamental meanings of the stages are identical.

Adding in the two new stages gives us eight stages which, in Maslow-leaning terminology, are as follows.

1. Survival - food and shelter are the focus of this first stage of consciousness.

2. Safety through grouping with others. This is the tribal stage of history, where groups of typically 150 people would band together and see other tribes as competitors for resources and therefore as enemies.

3. Courage. A new stage which adds onto Maslow's original work.. Courage brings the desire for exploration, competitive behavior, and for seeking dominance through sports or combat. In its negative form, it can manifest as predator consciousness or bullying.

4. Belonging - social acceptance and respect from others, a desire for purpose, status and recognition within an ordered social hierarchy. In its negative form, a sense of judgment runs rampant.

5. Intellect. Gaining self-confidence through intellectual development and achievement leading to freedom through independence. In its negative form, this stage can manifest as an inflated sense of ego.

6. Compassion. The other new stage which adds onto Maslow's original work. Compassion - or harmony through heart consciousness - brings about a spirit of cooperation and a caring sense of service to the community. It also invokes an aesthetic need for beauty and harmony. The compassion of this stage of consciousness frees one from a sense of wanting to judge others.

7. Self-Actualization - achieving one's unique potential, following one's highest joy to align with one's higher purpose and experience the higher aspect of heart consciousness and its ability to sense the universal supply of unconditional love

8. Transcendence - spiritual awakening through the inner experience of oneness with the universe and all life

Heart-Powered Consciousness Defined

In my first book, *The Shift: The Revolution in Human Consciousness*, I pointed out how these stages or memes correspond exactly to the stages of consciousness in the human chakra system. Chakras are gateways of consciousness, each one an *energy vortex* specializing in its own frequency. They are lenses through which your awareness flows. At any moment, you make a choice as to whether the frequency of your thoughts will be routine and mundane or something higher.

There are seven major chakras in the human subtle energy system but they have a total of twelve faces:

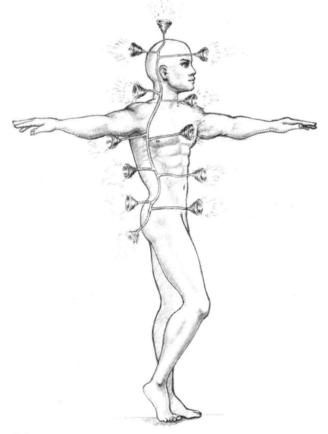

The top and the bottom chakras are both singular in nature, while the other five chakras each have two faces. In each case, one face is forward-facing in front of the body while the other is backward-facing. Both faces spring from their individual connections to the spinal area.

For example, the solar plexus (navel) chakra has two faces. The forward-facing solar plexus chakra has the characteristic of searching for order and purpose in life, just like meme number four. The backward-facing solar plexus chakra resonates exactly one musical half-tone higher in frequency and has the characteristic of striving to succeed in personal achievement, just like meme number five.

My book, *The Shift*, details my research on how the twelve potential memes of social progress correlate exactly with the twelve half-tones of the musical octave and also with the twelve faces of the seven major chakras. Social science has so far only recognized the first eight of the twelve stages of human consciousness because they are the only ones that have been observed in enough abundance so far to be able to form conclusions as to their nature.

It is inspiring to know that there are four more stages of enlightened consciousness available to us above the previously recognized eight stages.

Society today is working through a variety of fears in its journey toward the next level of consciousness. This next step is heart-centered consciousness and it is associated with meme number six, the receptive, sensitive, forward face of the heart chakra.

Once people discover the freedom of heart-centered consciousness, the next step is what Professor Clare Graves called "a momentous leap" into the second tier of six memes. While the first tier of six memes is one of basic consciousness, the next tier is one of spiritual awareness. By stepping from stage six's **heart-centered** consciousness to stage seven's **heart-powered** consciousness, each individual reaches stage or meme number seven, the first meme in that second, spiritual tier.

A world in transformation may seem chaotic at times because change causes much turbulence. Looking at consciousness as energy, when an established pattern is disturbed by a rise in frequency, a choppy pattern appears - one which is searching for a new form. At this time, personal and societal discords can abound as old wounds arise seeking attention and resolution. As the frequency of consciousness rises even more towards the new level, the unsettled patterns morph into an entirely new pattern, one which is even more complex and beautiful than the original one it replaces.

People reach heart-centered consciousness, the initial, meme six stage of heart consciousness in their own time. Then, they take that next step into stage seven, entering the spiritual tier of memes to experience the energy and drive of meme seven's heart-powered consciousness.

With stage seven's heart-powered consciousness comes the inspiration of a deeper sense of intuition, the emotional rewards of unconditional love, and a newfound level of inner creativity.

With inspiration, love and creativity, a new dimension of living is born, one which can truly help to create a new and better, heart-powered world.

The world is changing. Welcome to the dawning New Reality!

The Yin-Yang Nature of the Chakras

When we look at the eight stages of consciousness in the Maslow-8 list and compare them to the faces of the human chakras, we can see a perfect correlation.

These same stages of consciousness are experienced in an evolving society and in an evolving individual. They are designed into the consciousness system of human beings as natural steps toward the ultimate purpose in life, that of reconnecting fully with one's innermost Divine nature.

Stage no, Name - facing direction   Function/Manifests as:

1. Root chakra...   Instinctual/Personal survival.

2. Sacral chakra – front... Emotional-receptive/Clannishness.
3. Sacral chakra – back... Emotional-active/Courage.

4. Solar plexus – front...   Intellectual-receptive/Ordered purpose.
5. Solar plexus – back...   Intellectual-active/Achievement.

6. Heart chakra – front...   Holistic-receptive/Caring community.
7. Heart chakra – back...   Holistic-active/Responsible freedom.

8. Throat chakra – front...Creative-receptive/Intuitive development

There is a yin-yang character to the front and back faces of a chakra. The front-facing chakra is more feeling-oriented (yin) while the back-facing chakra is more expressive in an individualistic way (yang).

The front-facing chakras are receptive - they receive energy from the environment. For example, when you enter a room full of people, you unconsciously sense the mood within the room through the front, receptive face of your solar plexus pair of chakras.

The back-facing chakras are active – they transmit energy to the environment after it has been conditioned by its path through the individual. In this way, each person's thoughts and feelings contribute to the atmosphere of the global mind.

For example, the front-facing heart chakra face is the yin (predominantly receptive face) of the heart chakra pair. The back-facing heart chakra face is the yang (predominantly active face) of the heart chakra pair.

As we progress in consciousness through the chakras, we first feel our way into a new chakra pair via its front face. Once we have absorbed its feeling into our emotions and our beings, then we turn to the active face of the chakra and begin to express those feelings in practical action.

Where the World Stands Today

The consciousness of the majority people in the developed world today is focused in Stage Five, where the intellect is used to achieve advances in personal and societal standing.

Some people still insist on focusing more on Stage Four, where rigid obedience to authoritarian systems reduces their potential for exploration and growth.

On the lower end of the scale, people in war-torn or riot-filled areas of the world find their level of consciousness forced down to the combative level of Stage Three and, when their safety is threatened, even further to the basic survival level of Stage One.

Maslow was right: You can't focus on higher ideals like self-actualization when your safety and survival is at risk. The basic needs have to be secure in order to reach and express your personal potential in life.

At the higher end of today's world consciousness, progressive people are exploring Stage Six, the first stage of heart consciousness which expresses as a sense of caring community.

Meanwhile, the leading edge of humanity regularly ventures into Stage Seven consciousness, which is the active phase of heart-powered consciousness.

Stage Seven expresses as a sense of Responsible Freedom and is key to your liberation from the distracting noise of today's turbulent eruptions of conflict.

Today, one has to be on constant guard against being pulled down by the pockets of negative mental atmosphere generated by others. If you allow it, this can drag you down into a place where your personal power shrinks along with your ability to positively influence the world.

For example, when people glimpse the heart-centered concerns of Stage Six they feel compassion for those who are being pulled down by the injustice of various bad actors in society. Now, here is the big test. Do you maintain your focus on higher consciousness, where you have the power to really help, or do you spiral down into Stage Three combative behavior and join in with the melee of using words as weapons to attack your newfound enemies?

That being the test, you must then ask: If your power to help the world is so much greater in levels of higher consciousness, how do you actually **DO something** that will really work for the benefit of the world? I'm so glad you asked... ☺

Here is one powerful and effective answer...

How to Activate Heart-Centered Consciousness

The first stage of heart chakra activation is heart-centered consciousness. It is most easily achieved using the power of gratitude. Giving thanks is the expression of gratitude, and gratitude is one of the most beautiful secrets in spiritual life.

Gratitude is an expression of love, and love is something which flows from the Creator of the universe through all forms of life and all forms of manifestation. Without love, life in the universe cannot exist. Love is the universal force of preservation which holds creation in manifestation.

The Natural Flow of Love

Love is as natural as the universe. By design, there is a tension between the forces of creation and universal love. It is this tension which controls the size of the universe, holding it within its envelope. It is this tension which regulates the size of an electron's orbit around a nucleus. It is Universal Love which forms the force of attraction which retains electrons in their orbits, making atoms possible and therefore the existence of life as we know it.

You can block love, or you can allow it to flow naturally through you. Falling in love with another person is an allowance of the flow of love through your heart. In a world where everything has the appearance of separateness, it is a surrender to the underlying unity of all life. It is a place of apparent vulnerability, a willingness to take the risk that the illusion of separation will once again return if that love is later lost.

When you allow your heart to open to the universe's flow of love, gratitude comes with that flow. Gratitude for being alive, for just existing, for just being in the flow of the adventure of life. Gratitude for the Sun that gives us life. Gratitude for the Earth that gives us our home in the cosmos. Gratitude for the people that you love, and for those who share your journey through life.

Gratitude flows unimpeded from an open heart. When you allow it, it flows as freely as the sunshine, unobstructed by judgments or conditions.

A great daily habit is to begin your morning quiet time by thinking of ten things for which you are grateful - for people in your life, for your skills and abilities, for the environment that supports you, for the opportunities for growth that life is presenting to you, and so on.

Or, simply use the following affirmation. Keep repeating it while, each time, thinking more and more of what the words mean.

It adds new meaning to the words, "Quality of life." It really works! Try it now…

Gratitude Affirmation

I am grateful for life
And all that I love
I am grateful for the Earth
And the Sun up above
I am grateful for my spirit
And my inner being
For the oneness that is within
And the joy of this feeling

The Global Mind Atmosphere

It was the psychology pioneer Carl Jung who first made it clear that the unconscious part of your mind is connected to - and affects - the collective consciousness of humanity.

This means that what you think and feel affects the whole of humanity, even though you are not consciously aware of that connection.

It also means that, the higher your frequency of consciousness, the more you *uplift* the collective consciousness of humanity.

There is an atmosphere of thoughts and feelings which surrounds the planet. Your conscious mind may not be actively aware of this global *mind belt*, but your subconscious mind is connected to it and your superconscious mind works with it all the time.

Your soul or superconscious mind helps you navigate life in the way most beneficial to you and it does this by hunches or inner feelings that point the way to the optimal solutions to problems that face you in your journey through life. It is able to do this because, from its perspective at a higher level of consciousness, it has a wider vista from which to see life's circumstances. It's like seeing the view from the mountaintop instead of the valley.

The mind belt of the planet consists of all frequencies of consciousness and resonates primarily to the average state of global consciousness. The more you raise your mind, the more the mind belt benefits from your contribution.

Mind energy consists of thoughts and feelings. It is a definite energy, even though it is much more subtle than physical energies like light or electricity. Mind energy is conditioned and directed by human will or intention.

You can be affected by waves of emotion springing up in the collective mind belt or you can decide for yourself how you will react to life's events. Choose now whether you will be affected by every twist and turn in the game of life, or whether you will be one of the few who create your own game.

Independent thinkers are the trendsetters in the mind belt. The way you think affects every other human upon the planet. The way you feel affects every other human upon the planet.

When you burn a pioneering trail into the mind belt, others will sense and follow your lead, amplifying the positive trend you initiated.

Develop your sense of unconditional love through regular, dedicated spiritual practices and you *will* change the world. From the perspective of your soul, at the end of the day, the one thing that counts the most is the amount of spiritual growth that you have achieved through your chosen experiences.

Your Lens Into the Mind Belt

People imagine that their thoughts are based in their brain, but that is only partly true. The brain processes physical information and provides you with the concepts of time and space so that you can function in the fabricated reality that appears to exist in a world outside of you.

Your mind, however, is a nonphysical field of consciousness and it is not fixed inside your head. Each of the seven major chakras, or energy centers associated with the human body, resonate to a specific frequency band of consciousness. For most people in today's world, daily thought is focused around the solar plexus chakra. In other words, your thoughts come from and through such a frequency lens or filter.

You receive mental energy from the global mind belt. Your thoughts and emotions condition this mind energy and you automatically re-transmit it back out into the mind belt. This can happen at the frequency of the solar plexus chakra or, in the case of higher thinking, at the frequency of the heart chakra.

At the lower end of solar plexus-level thinking, conditions of hierarchical control are experienced while, at the higher end, the focus becomes intellectual achievement. A century ago, when the world shifted from the authoritarian lens of the lower part of the solar plexus chakra toward the intellectual achievement of the higher part, a distinct sense of self-empowerment unfolded. Science, being an intellectual pursuit, was then able to progress by leaps and bounds.

A century ago, people used to accept the idea of obedience and unquestioning faith in spiritual dogma. Today, most people have grown to realize that they can think for themselves and create a lifestyle more ideally suited to the uniqueness of their own specific purpose in life.

The evolution of your consciousness produces an expansion in the size of your mind. The terms, "expanded consciousness" or "personal growth" literally refer to an expansion in the size of your mental field.

With the ongoing shift to New Reality thinking, the lens through which people see the world is moving from the solar plexus to the heart chakra. Heart-centered consciousness begins with an expansion of awareness that includes the needs of others and then progresses into the first stage of spiritual awakening.

People live within a chakra-related bubble of consciousness. Imagine it being rather like a deep sea diver's helmet or a spacesuit helmet. That bubble is moving up from the solar plexus level and the world is seen as a very different place when viewed from the more expansive, heart-centered perspective.

Looking through *the lens of the heart*, everything has a different perspective. Instead of providing an understanding of the emerging New Reality from a simply intellectual viewpoint, this viewpoint engages your higher feelings and the New Reality becomes a personal experience, not just a mental concept.

The Universal Supply of Unconditional Love

The purpose of being human, as we shift into the New Reality, is to learn about heart-centered consciousness.

The universe is, by its very design, filled with the love of the Original Creator. Universal love is the aspect of Original Consciousness which holds Creation together. In the Original Creation, Divine consciousness was divided into two complementary aspects – thought and feeling – and then set into motion.

The love of the Original Creator forms the very fabric of space. No material thing and no part of "empty" space is devoid of that love. Universal love is literally everywhere. However, the human condition is only affected by this all-pervasive universal love when it is channeled into the human realm through its use by humans.

We are here on Earth to learn how to translate universal love into human form.

Once universal love has been transformed through the consciousness of any individual human being, it enters the global mind atmosphere which is connected to all humans. We all share constant access to this global mind. While we initiate thoughts and feelings on our own, we also receive thoughts and feelings from the global mind. We sometimes alter these by our own thought, sometimes not, and then pass them back into the global mind.

Even though we are typically not accustomed to conscious telepathy, our subconscious and superconscious minds are fully telepathic. We constantly receive and transmit thoughts and feelings subconsciously from and to the global mind atmosphere.

When a person experiences heart-centered consciousness, they radiate a type of consciousness which is very different to basic emotion. Heart-centered consciousness is a state of unconditional love. It is not a product of emotional like or dislike. Once started, nothing in physical reality affects the flow of unconditional love.

Unconditional love is something that just is, regardless of the circumstances.

It is something that flows through your heart when you reach up above day-to-day consciousness, tune into your heart-awareness and allow the universal love energy to flow through you. Heart-centered consciousness always sees the elegant solution to the sorrows that can arise from basic human emotions.

Unconditional love allows, accepts, and supports. It is not something you *try* to do. It just *flows* when you allow it to enter your heart and take your consciousness above the cares of daily reality and into an expanded vista of awareness.

Each time you radiate unconditional love into the global mind atmosphere, you upgrade the entire human experience, taking humanity yet one more step into the unfolding New Reality.

Stepping Into Heart-Powered Transformation

After activating heart-centered consciousness, perhaps using gratitude as a stepping stone, the next stage is to step up into heart-powered consciousness.

This is where you imitate the Sun!

Well, okay, maybe you don't turn into a physical ball of light but, just like the Sun, you do radiate spiritual light for the benefit of others.

The ethic of the higher stage of heart consciousness is *service to others*. This empowers your spiritual progress in contrast to the service-to-self ethic common to solar plexus thinking, which creates conflicts and slows the evolution of the mind and spirit.

Speaking of the Sun, at this point it would be best to clarify its true function.

The True Nature of the Sun

One of the crowning achievements of modern science, arguably for better or worse, has been to understand the nature of nuclear fission. There is also progress being made to create far less toxic electric power generators using nuclear fusion, not fission. Scientists believe that the Sun uses nuclear fusion to slowly transform hydrogen into helium, producing light, heat, and other electromagnetic energies for the benefit of the solar system.

The metaphysical point of view is more all-encompassing: The Sun is a step-down transformer of energies from a higher dimension of existence. These energies are compressed so that they can serve our particular density of existence. There are not only electromagnetic energies, but also etheric (life energy or qi) energies as well as mental, emotional (universal love), and spiritual frequencies of energy.

These energies arrive courtesy of a series of step-down transformations, starting with the Creator and the (higher-dimensional) Central Sun of the universe, then moving through the central sun of each galaxy, and then through the suns of each solar system. These energies are consumed by all forms of life in the universe and, when spent, they are eventually recycled back through black holes for recharging and re-use by the Creator.

Becoming a Beacon of Light

Service to others - being inspired by the Sun to act as a beacon of light to help humanity - is an act of world healing. The question is, how do you practice an effective form of world healing?

Here is a fundamental technique for healing the world by attracting, conditioning, and radiating spiritual energy. It is essential that you pause here long enough to try this technique for yourself. If you just read about it and avoid trying it out, you will miss the experience of its liberating effects upon your mind, body and spirit.

Exercise: Sit upright with your hands resting in your lap, palms facing upwards. Breathe rhythmically and evenly. Turn away from your everyday thoughts by letting your attention focus on your breath. Whenever you notice your thoughts wandering, peacefully turn away from those thoughts, which can always be dealt with later, and return to focusing on your breath.

Heart-centered consciousness is focused in the heart chakra, or energy center, which is located approximately four inches (ten centimeters) in front of the breastbone. Like all chakras, the front-facing heart chakra is a small, whirling vortex of energy operating at a specific frequency of consciousness.

Universal life energy, or etheric energy, comes from the universe, through the Sun, and fills all of the space around you. On a sunny day, when its presence is especially intense, your eyes can often faintly detect globules of this energy floating in the air as you look up towards the clear sky.

Universal life energy responds immediately to applied mental pressure, so you can use your imagination to apply mental pressure to attract, condition, and radiate this etheric form of energy. We will be using this energy as a carrier wave for our mental and spiritual intentions.

Intend world healing by visualizing positive changes in the world. Even though you are healing something that you may perceive as negative, it is important to focus instead on the desired positive outcome. If you send energy to something negative, you could amplify its power. By sending energy to something positive, you make that form of healing possible.

In your mind's eye, instead of a world suffering from strife, visualize the people of the world at peace. Instead of spiritual ignorance and the suffering that it prolongs, visualize people who are becoming enlightened by spiritual understanding. Instead of seeing people displaced and distraught from a recent catastrophe, see what's needed – aid workers being successful in their efforts to bring relief and assistance to the area.

Now, return your attention to your breathing. With every inbreath, see your lungs being filled with the vibrant white light of the universal life energy which fills the air around you.

With every outbreath, send the power of this love and light out to humanity. Direct it as a beam of *brilliant* white light from your heart chakra out into the world.

Perform this as a series of inbreaths and outbreaths for as long as you wish, then relax and spend some time in the afterglow of a spiritual mission well accomplished.

These are the days of action, and that means service to others. Even better, your service to others also helps you in your own spiritual enlightenment. Action and reaction are opposite and equal. By helping others, you help yourself.

Every time you send your light out into the world, you take another step forward toward your own enlightenment.

In summary, this World Healing Technique is as follows:

* Sit upright with your eyes closed.
* Make a spiritual connection, one which includes gratitude for life.
* Intend world healing by visualizing the desired positive outcome.
* Breathe in universal life energy with each inbreath.
* On each outbreath, repeat your intention and send a beam of white light from the energy center of your heart to your intended destination.

The Power of Focus in Spiritual Work

When troubles are close to home, focus down to concentrate the effect of your efforts. Instead of spreading your efforts to the world in general, focus locally - on your home, your street, your community. Then, you can make magic happen.

How You Are Already Healing the World

When you raise your frequency of consciousness to embrace higher states, you heal, not only yourself, but the world as a whole!

Now, you might ask what significant effect one solitary person could have upon a planet-wide mind belt which is connected into by billions of people. The answer to that question was discovered by Map of Consciousness pioneer David R Hawkins. He found that the scale of consciousness is not linear; it is exponential. It goes up the scale, not in a straight line, but in *multiples* with every step up the frequency ladder.

Higher frequencies of consciousness have an enormously multiplied influence on the mind belt. And, because the effect is exponential, your uplifting thoughts can *counter-balance* the effects of *hundreds and even hundreds of thousands* of people who are engaged in a depressing struggle for basic existence at the lower end of the consciousness spectrum!

Because higher frequencies of thought and feeling have proportionately more power than lower frequency ones, the unconditional love that you generate through your spiritual practices has a huge influence upon humanity.

Imagine, as one person, having the effect of thousands of people in uplifting the mind belt connected to all humanity!

There is hope for a better world, even when the few seek to raise the mind belt to a better place. *The few* really do have the power to raise the many.

Hawkins set up a system of calibrating levels of human consciousness. Assigning the numbers one to infinity as the possible range of consciousness, he soon found that he had to use the logarithm of numbers, rather than just plain numbers, to cater for their exponential nature. This is because the power of consciousness at higher levels is vast compared to its power at lower levels.

When you use a base-ten logarithmic system, the number 4 is not twice the number 2. Log 4 is 10,000 (one plus four zeros) versus log 2's value of just 100 (one plus two zeros). A consciousness level of 300 is not twice 150, it is 10 to the 300th power; a one with 300 zeros after it.

Furthermore, Hawkins found that the consciousness level of 200 was critical. A global average of 200 or more is necessary to sustain life on this planet without it sinking into eventual self-destruction. Since the mid-1980s, he reports, the global average reading for humanity climbed above the critical 200 level. This, of course, is yet another discovery confirming the existence of today's ongoing shift in consciousness.

Then, he began to wonder how much people of higher consciousness were compensating for people who live below the 200 level. Consider, for example, that 800 million people in the world are hungry, with many of them living near starvation. The consciousness of despair tests at a level of just 50. Even anger and hatred rate higher in frequency than the deep depression experienced by those who live with no appearance of hope.

So here we are, on Planet Earth, a collective humanity swimming hard through life to keep our collective chins above the 200 level, working towards the day when hunger and hopelessness will be eradicated from our world once and for all.

What can you do to help? As you raise your consciousness, you contribute more and more to the spiritual quality of the global mind. Therefore, your greatest service to humanity is, paradoxically, the development of your own consciousness.

How exactly can that help the world? Getting back to modern science and its numbering systems, along with today's liking for summaries that spell out 'the bottom line,' here are the test results.

One individual at a higher level of consciousness counterbalances many, many individuals who are below the critical level of 200. Below the 200 level are the attractor fields of shame, guilt, apathy, grief, fear, desire, anger and pride. Right at the critical 200 level comes courage and its ability to empower the self out of the victim-orientation of the lower frequencies.

At 300, a person has risen above many emotions of conflict to achieve some non-judgment and to feel optimism. At 300, one person, within the global mind, counterbalances an incredible total of 90,000 people below the 200 level. Such is the power of higher states of consciousness.

At 400, the individual achieves a harmonious attitude which brings acceptance and forgiveness. Furthermore, they gain an enhanced sense of reason, which brings understanding and meaning to life. This is not a difficult level to achieve. Those who, for example, pursue higher education and the professions function at the 400 level, where one person counterbalances an incredible 400,000 people below the 200 level.

To reach 500, a person needs to be spiritually conscious. At this level, unconditional love and unconditional forgiveness become alive and well in their reality. Here, one person counterbalances 750,000 people who are below the 200 level.

When a person has practiced meditation long and diligently enough to attain bliss consciousness at the 600 level, they are, at that moment, counterbalancing 10 million people below the 200 level.

Do you need a more compelling reason to develop your inner faculties? Just look at the wonderful level of service that each advance in consciousness brings into our world.

And all this is by just being who you are and who you can become, before you even begin to physically help make the world a better place through your support and direct action. This wonderful level of service is the direct effect of your consciousness upon a world which has been starved, for so long, of spiritual thought and spiritual energy.

Intuitive Development

One of the great side effects of daily exposure to Stage Seven heart-powered consciousness is that it steadily develops your intuitive ability. Intuition is a faculty based in Stage Eight consciousness, which is Maslow's ultimate level of Transcendence.

Inspiring, helpful ideas come from your superconscious mind into your conscious mind through the sense of intuition. They are subtle whispers rather than loud and clear messages, so it takes practice to recognize them and not just let them pass through unnoticed.

Intuitive hunches can arrive as a knowingness about something or, sometimes, just a feeling that leans toward a certain direction, suggesting a better choice. The signals are always subtle because the superconscious mind is based in a more subtle (and therefore less limited) realm of existence than the physical world.

Women may be more familiar with the sense of intuition, but it flows equally through men and women, provided you allow it and encourage it. Intuition is a sense of knowingness. It's what makes a person say, "I just know." It's a sense beyond the physical senses.

Intuition comes from your soul-level or superconscious mind to help you navigate life in the way most beneficial to your own unique path through life. Your inner being - your immortal soul - has a wider vista from which to see life's circumstances. Your soul level of consciousness, being essentially *you*, knows more about your true needs than any guide or counselor could ever know.

Your inner being is aware of much more than the five senses that feed into the conscious mind. It is aware of the underlying consciousness of situations and of all the people, objects, thoughts and feelings relating to those situations.

It knows ahead of time if a problem will crop up and it can see the best way to either handle it or avoid it entirely. Such is the value of intuitive information and this is a compelling reason to develop one's ability to consciously receive such insights.

Intuition can bring you direct information about any object or situation, anywhere, and from any time – past, present or future.

Good intuition gives you superconscious help.

The Principle of Spiritual Energy Generation

As people become more interested in spirituality and how it can change the world and improve their lives, the understanding of spiritual energy becomes a key factor in their growth and development. This article explains the nature of spiritual energy and how it can be used in, for example, distance healing, world healing, or simply for enhancing meditation.

Like the principle of electrical generation, the principle of spiritual energy generation shows how a specific type of energy flow may be generated. In the case of electrical generation, a flow of electricity is created in a certain direction. In the case of spiritual energy generation, a flow of spiritual energy is created in a certain direction.

Spiritual energy is universal etheric life energy conditioned by spiritual intent.

Etheric energy is a primary energy of the universe, while electric energy is a secondary, more dense form of energy. Etheric energy is also known by many other names around the world, including life energy, vital energy, prana, bioenergy, orgone, ki, chi or qi.

Etheric energy is no stranger to anyone. In fact, it's as close as your fingertips. When seen against a light background with your eyes out of focus, etheric energy surrounds the ends of your fingertips like a ghostly aura.

For the last 5,000 years in traditional Chinese medicine, the vital pathways of etheric energy in the human body have been balanced using the healing modality of acupuncture. More recently, the electrical genius Nikola Tesla produced vast quantities of etheric energy using, apparently, very high frequency electricity as a method of attracting etheric energy out of the atmosphere. Because its behavior is very different from regular electricity, he referred to it as 'cold electricity.'

Just as the atmosphere is filled with electrons, ready to be channeled through an electric generator, so is it also filled with etheric energy. All energies are supplied and replenished by the Sun, including the mental energy that forms the global mind atmosphere or mind belt around the Earth.

The mind belt is conditioned by the thoughts and emotions of humankind. Each person constantly attracts mental energy, conditions it by their thoughts and actions, and passes it back into the mind belt. Every one of us affects everyone else. A spiritual act – one which expresses unconditional love – by anyone anywhere upon the planet improves the mind belt of the whole planet.

Etheric energy is a more subtle energy than electricity, and a more dense energy than mental energy. However, because of its vibrational proximity to mental energy, it responds readily to applied mental pressure. In other words, mental visualization can be used to apply pressure to direct etheric energy.

The human mind can, through visualization and intent, attract etheric energy, condition it in any way desired, and then direct it towards any desired objective.

Both electric energy and etheric energy respond to pressure. In the case of electrical energy, voltage is the measure of electrical pressure. The more voltage you can create, the more electrical energy you can move through a circuit. In the case of etheric energy, the application of pressure via mental intent is similar to the principle of voltage. As a higher form of energy, etheric energy responds readily to mental pressure.

The more intense your intention, the more etheric energy you will move toward your intended objective. For example, if you are sending distance healing energy to a friend at another location, the stronger the pressure of your applied intent, the more healing energy you can generate and transfer to them.

Spiritual energy is etheric energy conditioned by spiritual intent. In order to achieve the spiritual conditioning of etheric energy and transform it into spiritual energy, the individual's consciousness has to first rise into the frequency range of spiritual consciousness.

In the human heart lies the doorway from material consciousness to spiritual consciousness. As explained in my book, *The Shift: The Revolution in Human Consciousness* and earlier in this book, there are two levels of heart-centered consciousness and they resonate at different frequencies. It's a yin and yang situation. The lower, passive level is heartfelt consciousness, where the person adjusts to the experience of unconditional love. The higher, active level is heart-powered consciousness, where the person puts that heart-centered awareness into action.

The Doorway to Spiritual Consciousness

The doorway to spiritual consciousness lies between those two levels of heart-centered awareness. There are two major tiers of human consciousness, each tier containing six stages. The basic tier has a materialistic focus and ranges from the earliest historical expression of human consciousness, all the way through the evolution of empowered action and achievement, and into heartfelt awareness. In this heartfelt state of consciousness, humans shift from supporting - for example, mindless commercial expansion - into an awareness where the environment becomes an important issue.

Humans then progress into the second tier of six stages of human evolution. This is the spiritual tier and, by stepping into it, humankind today is making a quantum leap in awareness. This is the essential nature of *The Shift* that is steadily transforming today's society. As each human spends more and more time in the spiritual tier, they engage in more and more heart-powered action, changing the world through applied unconditional love.

The average person in Western society today is still in the commercial expansion stage of consciousness, and yet with one foot very much planted in the heartfelt consciousness of ecology issues. Meanwhile, today's pioneers of The Shift are spending more and more time venturing into the spiritual tier of consciousness and, as a result, expanding the awareness of all of humanity.

In Summary

The generation of spiritual energy is carried out through spiritual intent applied to the universal supply of etheric energy. The spiritual tier of consciousness begins with heart-powered consciousness and is entered through the doorway of the heart. The degree of intent determines the amount of etheric energy that will be conditioned into spiritual energy. Intent is also used to direct the spiritual energy towards the desired objective, such as distance healing, world healing, or simply for enhancing meditation.

The Principle of Spiritual Energy Generation states that spiritual energy is generated by the mental direction of etheric energy, conditioned by spiritual intent.

Becoming More of Your True Self

Traditionally, society has pressured people into conformity. Peer pressure to conform to an immediate social group begins at school because, from an early age, people are taught that they should conform to outside standards.

In England, the phrase "know your place" is used as a put-down to someone who has started to become outstanding in some way. In Australia, the traditional phrase is "cut down the tall poppies." In Japan, it is "The nail that sticks up shall be pounded down."

However, this pressure towards conformity has been lessening in recent decades, and it will continue to lessen as people realize that there is strength in diversity. Diversity is natural. Conformity is unnatural. In the universe, every snowflake, every person, and even every proton is unique. Together, the sum of the parts makes up a perfect universe of infinite diversity.

Diversity is designed into the universe because the universe exists in order that Infinite Being, the All That Is, may gain an infinite variety of experiences. In the case of human beings as expressions of the one source, we have freewill so that we can makes choices. Making choices, and experiencing the results of those choices, is what human life is all about.

Inner alignment means becoming more of your true self. Your inner being is your true self, and by developing your inner potential, you express more and more of your true self. In heart-centered, New Reality consciousness, mutual support is shared between people. That means that being different is good, developing personal skills is good, and exploring your own potential is good. Deep within, everyone is equal. However, in your unique form of expression in the outer world, you are different to everyone else. Not better or worse, not more-than or less-than; just different, because diversity is natural and is honored through mutual respect.

The New Reality of heart-centered consciousness is being built on this Earth, one person at a time. New Reality consciousness is a supportive and empowered state of consciousness, rather than the Old Reality consciousness of separation and fear.

Imagine a transformation in the workplace where, instead of the enormous amount of energy today consumed by office politics to "keep the competition down," people acted like true teams - supportive of each other's strengths and encouraging their development so that each team can gain as these strengths develop and diversify to tackle ever-greater challenges.

This is no great mystery. It's called a win-win situation. Everyone gains when fear is put aside and energies are used constructively instead of negatively, and it happen with just one step up from solar plexus awareness to heart-centered awareness.

When a person manifests their own unique, inner being, they become aligned, in the way that a laser beam is aligned, rather than being scattered by external should's and should-not's. A beam of laser light is powerful because it is coherent, not scattered in different directions. Your outer consciousness becomes more powerful when it is aligned with your inner being, not scattered in different directions. When many people in society become aligned in their own personal power, the whole becomes far more influential than the sum of the parts. In fact, it becomes exponentially more powerful.

When enough pioneers choose New Reality consciousness, there will come a day when their powerfully-aligned influence will reach a critical mass. Then, it will transform the remainder of society and, suddenly, everyone will "get it." Society, as a whole, will then realize that heart-centered consciousness is the way forward into creating its bright, new future.

Magic Happens

As your spiritual practices progress, you find that, more and more, magic seems to happen around you. That is because you are becoming more and more attuned to the Divine source within you. You can call this God, The Universe, or Source; it matters not. Words are inadequate to describe the presence of Infinite Being, the universal awareness behind all life. But, the more you attune to that essence, the more life unfolds in an ideal way. Problems dissolve and elegant solutions become apparent for previously insurmountable challenges.

The Spiritualize Technique uses this principle to transform your life into a happier, more healthful, and more inspired reality. It encapsulates ways of reaching higher consciousness which are so effective that, for centuries, they were suppressed and driven underground. Today, as we experience a world of rapid change and a planetary shift to higher consciousness, the secrets are out. They are available right now, without any barrier blocking your way, and they are ready to help you transform your life for the better. This is a spiritual development technique that will act as an anchor of stability and inspiration in the fast-changing 21st century.

The question is, are you ready for the transformational power of the Spiritualize technique? The one barrier that could still prevent you from gaining such spiritual growth is the one that you can erect yourself. Can you believe the truth about the enormous spiritual power that resides within you? The truth is, we ALL have that power within us.

The deeper our sciences probe into the nature of physical matter, the more apparent it becomes that everything in this world is connected to everything else. To outward appearances, we have individual identity and appear to be separate from each other but, in reality, we are connected to all matter and to all people. This is because every person is a unique facet of the same all-pervasive intelligence. You are not connected to God or the "All That Is" like an add-on module, you are God in expression because everything in existence is an expression of the mind of God. We have different viewpoints of reality but we are all representations of the One, the Divine, or the great Presence that exists within all things.

Your mind may need time to get used to the true nature of the Divinity within you, but that alone is no barrier to success. Practice the Spiritualize technique regardless of any temporary doubt you may harbor. Just do it regardless. Let it work for you and you will experience its transformative power. As that happens, any doubt will evaporate in the light of experience and you will have the most powerful tool ever for transforming your life into a happier, more healthful, and more inspired reality.

When you enter a sufficiently higher state of consciousness, life's challenges become transformed.

Problem situations can become solved through the correct practice of this technique in one of two ways: Either by being energetically healed and transformed or by an inspired solution becoming apparent.

The primary purpose of the Spiritualize technique is to give you a way to anchor your mind to the reality within at any time of the day. By attuning with your Divine connection, you rise above the turmoil and illusion of events in the outside world. True reality is within the higher part of you. The more you connect with your higher consciousness, the more inspired and successful your life becomes. The main purpose of human life is spiritual growth. This is how you can make your spiritual growth happen each and every day.

Principles of the Spiritualize Technique

1) You are one with God. You are an individualized aspect of the consciousness of the Creator charged with the mission of experiencing life from one unique point of view. By consciously aligning yourself with the Divine Presence behind all things, you invoke its transformative power.

2) The universe is completely benevolent. God is good. Any appearance of evil in this world is caused by a lack of spiritual light, just as shadow or coldness is caused by a lack of physical light. All beings are inherently drawn to finding their inner light and everyone succeeds in this, their primary motivation, sooner or later. By consciously realizing the goodness of God, we open our eyes and see the light. The appearance of any darkness then disappears.

3) Action creates results. Transformation occurs when you raise your consciousness sufficiently. When you elevate yourself into a state of higher consciousness through this technique, your situation becomes transformed by the goodness and harmony of God's universal energies. The key point to realize is that the responsibility for action begins with you as the physical anchor within any situation. When you align yourself sufficiently with the presence of God and the benevolent nature of all Creation, all things in your life can transform and become healed. It is the realization of your oneness with the Divine and the realization of the goodness of God that acts as a transformative power within your reality.

The Spiritualize Technique –
Quick, Simple, Powerful

The Spiritualize technique contains powerful principles which help you to connect easily and quickly with the transformative power of the Divine Presence. Once you are thoroughly familiar with the technique and have used it many times, you will find it becomes a part of you.

First, detach from any thoughts of problems that need attention.
Your higher consciousness is fully aware of all of your situation. Any conscious attachment to any pressing needs will hold your mind down in the physical world, so detach completely from all concerns for the duration of this practice.

Focus on your breathing while your body relaxes and your mind settles into a reflective state. Then, take three heart-breaths as follows: On each inbreath, visualize spiritual energy as an intense white light coming from the Sun, all the way through space and then filling your brain. On each outbreath, transfer that energy down the spine to the level of the heart, then send it out the front of your body into your heart chakra, which is a vortex of energy located approximately four inches (ten centimeters) in front of the breastbone.

Your heart chakra is the gateway to spiritual consciousness. You connect to the God space through your heart space.

Then, silently make these declarations:

I am in God.
God is in me.
God and I are one.

Note: This is the use of the word "God" in its deepest sense. It refers to Infinite Being, the awareness behind the conscious universe. If you would prefer another term to God, the possibilities include The Universe, Brahman, Tao, and The Absolute.

For a moment, think about these statements and what the realization of Oneness means to you. Feel the closeness of the Presence of God with every breath you take and every beat of your heart. Feel the Presence right there with you as a living reality. Continue to focus on the breath in order to reach the necessary state of peace and deep relaxation. Notice how the breath brings a state of peace and serenity. Once you have reached this peaceful state, you no longer focus on the breath. Stop thinking and listen.

Adopt a state of attentive silence. Be receptive to the still, silent voice of inner awareness. It is important to be mentally still and allow the sense of the Divine Presence. Once you start actively thinking again, the experience is over. Mental chatter stops the process, so be attentive and adopt a state of expectancy. The secret is in the stillness.

At first, you may not hear anything, but you will experience, if only through a deep breath or inner sigh, the Presence. It is the moment of connection that is important. Then you have completed the purpose of that session.

You may receive information and insights during the process or they may come later. As you practice, you develop your ability to "hear". Some people receive impressions as mental pictures, some hear them as mental words, but most people simply receive ideas as a sudden arrival of understanding. The wisdom from your soul will be able to reach you either at this moment or at a later time while your attention is diverted elsewhere. Be especially attentive in the next few hours for any subtle idea that arises more than once. It is the repetitive occurrence of such thoughts into your conscious mind that alert you to the realization that you are receiving a suggestion worthy of immediate consideration.

When you feel the peace of the Presence, you have opened yourself to God as Infinite Intelligence. This Infinite Intelligence knows your every need and, by realizing this, you have opened the doors for that realization to express Itself.

The Spiritualize technique fits into any busy schedule. Practice it at the start of every day in order to prompt intuitive support for the day ahead. Use it several times a day whenever you need inner guidance or whenever an existing problem jumps into your mind. It takes just one to five minutes.

Throughout your day, you will be turning within and aligning with the truth of your being. Several times on a daily basis, you will be connecting with a higher level of consciousness, spiritualizing all aspects of your life. By using it throughout your day, you begin to train yourself to focus on Reality rather than illusion. This opens up the resources of your inner world so that your outer world will reflect this higher understanding and wisdom.

The Essential Steps of the Spiritualize Technique

1. Focus inward. You must turn your attention within as God is within you. Nothing is 'out there' except the illusion of matter and your outward performance in the theater of life.

2. Breathe into your heart chakra. Heart-centered consciousness is the gateway to God. If you use your intellect only, you will be unable to proceed to step 3.

3. Connect with God. Leave behind all your cares and the issues of the day. Focus your thoughts only upon God. Then stop thinking, be still, and listen. This will have a transformative effect upon your situation and your life.

A Deep Secret Revealed

As a parting thought, here is a secret that, until recent times, was heavily guarded by the enlightened adepts. Today, that information is open to public view for your benefit.

When you wish to affect physical objects and the physical world, you speak your words out loud.

When you wish to affect the mind belt as it applies to your situation, you whisper your words so quietly that someone right next to you can hardly hear what you are saying.

When you wish to affect only the spiritual reality around you, such as when you are asking for higher inspiration, you *think* the words while curling the tip of your tongue back so that you can push the base of your tongue firmly against the roof of your mouth. This locks the tongue in place so that it cannot move with any physical expression of the words you say mentally, thus assuring the energy goes above the mental level and focuses on the spiritual level of consciousness.

Now, you truly do have a way to make magic happen around you.

The Most Productive Daily Habit

Be prepared to remind yourself each day of your true spiritual nature in order to insulate yourself from the constant daily supply of negative conditioning that typically comes with life on earth today.

In order to maintain higher consciousness on a daily basis, it is vital that you engage in a daily spiritual practice session.

The best time for a daily quiet time is first thing in the morning. If you have to be somewhere at a certain time each morning, plan your sleep time 15 minutes earlier.

Start a new habit. It will be the most rewarding habit of the day because, just like rose-tinted glasses, it raises your whole experience of everything that happens that day.

Start your morning session by thinking of ten things for which you are grateful. Use the Spiritualize Technique or a meditation technique of your choosing. The final and most important part of your session should be World Healing. That *really* gets your energy moving in the way that God intended for all spiritually-minded beings.

Then, have a beautiful day!

About the Author

Owen Waters is an international spiritual teacher who has presented his insights into the New Reality to hundreds of thousands of seekers. In 1963, at the age of just thirteen, he encountered his first spiritual awakening. The surprise of this mystical experience was such that his life became focused upon a continuous search for spiritual answers.

Almost forty years of study and research followed, along with the development of his inner vision. By the year 2002, like many of the spiritual teachers who are coming forward to help with today's shift in consciousness, his realizations began to unfold rapidly.

Today, as co-founder of the Spiritual Dynamics Academy, he promotes a philosophy of spiritual empowerment through inner connection to the source of ultimate human potential.

Be sure to sign up for his free Sunny Sundays newsletter, where each issue contains an inspiring article on spiritual growth at www.SpiritualDynamics.net

Made in the USA
Middletown, DE
12 December 2021